DUDLEY SCH... KU-798-684

LIBRARY SERVICE

Ice Storms

DUNCAN SCHEFF

Nature on the Rampage

www.raintreepublishers.co.uk

Visit our website to find out more information about **Raintree** books.

To order:
☎ Phone 44 (0) 1865 888112
🖹 Send a fax to 44 (0) 1865 314091
💻 Visit the Raintree Bookshop at www.raintreepublishers.co.uk to browse our catalogue and order online.

First published in Great Britain by Raintree Publishers, Halley Court, Jordan Hill, Oxford, OX2 8EJ, part of Harcourt Education. Raintree is a registered trademark of Harcourt Education Ltd.

© Harcourt Education Ltd 2003

Raintree Publishers
Editor: Isabel Thomas
Production: Jonathan Smith
Cover design: Jo Sapwell and Michelle Lisseter

Originated by Dot Gradations
Printed and bound in China and Hong Kong by South China

ISBN 1 844 21213 0
07 06 05 04 03
10 9 8 7 6 5 4 3 2 1

British Library Cataloguing in Publication Data
Scheff, Duncan
Ice Storms. – (Nature on the Rampage)
1.Ice Storms – Juvenile literature
2.Hailstorms – Juvenile literature
551.5'54
A full catalogue for this book is available from the British Library

Acknowledgements
The publishers would like to thank the following for permission to reproduce photographs:
Digital Stock, p. **23**. Photodisk, p. **26**. Photo Network/Whiteley, p. **17**. Root Resources/Doug Sherman, pp. **1, 4, 8, 12, 25**; Mary Root, p. **20**. Visuals Unlimited/ Glen M. Oliver, p. **10**; Jeff J. Daly, p. **18**; John Gerlach, p. **29**

Cover photograph by Topham Picturepoint/Imageworks

Contents

These hailstones have fallen to the ground during a hailstorm.

The icy Earth

Ice and hail storms are the most harmful forms of **precipitation**. Precipitation is any form of moisture that falls from the sky. Ice storms and hailstorms pelt the ground with different forms of water. In an ice storm, rain falls as a liquid, but it freezes when it strikes cold objects or cold ground.

In a hailstorm, chunks of ice called hailstones fall from the sky. The chunks of ice must be at least 5 millimetres across for them to be called hailstones. If they are smaller than this, they are officially called soft hail. Hailstones can be much larger than 5 millimetres. Some are as large as tennis balls. The heaviest hailstones ever recorded weighed over a kilogram. They killed 92 people in Bangladesh during a storm on 14 April 1986.

About ice storms and hailstorms

Ice storms usually strike during cold weather. They are especially common in the winter in places like the northern USA and Canada. Ice storms coat everything with ice. The thickness of the ice depends on how much freezing rain falls. As the coat of ice gets thicker, it also gets heavier. Heavy ice causes problems. Freezing rain sometimes covers telephone wires with ice. The poles can break from the weight, and people lose telephone services. Ice can also make electricity cables and large tree branches collapse.

In an ice storm, clear sheets of ice may cover roads. This makes it hard to drive safely. Drivers may not see the clear ice that forms on roads. Because of the ice, they cannot stop or turn easily. This leads to road accidents.

Ice storms can injure or even kill animals. Cattle can die when ice freezes around their noses until they cannot breathe. Freezing rain can freeze birds' feet to tree branches and cats' paws to the ground.

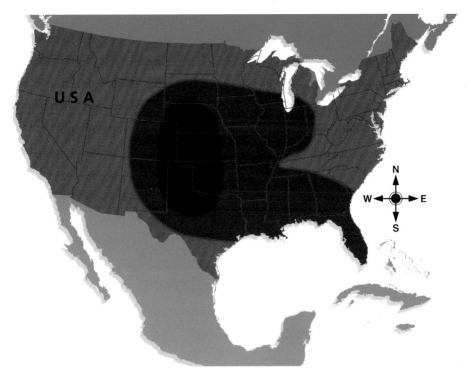

● common areas for thunderstorms
● Hail Alley

▲ This map shows the location of Hail Alley, where hailstorms often strike.

Hail is formed inside storm clouds. Hailstorms usually happen in the spring or summer, but they can strike at any time of the year. They occur almost anywhere that conditions are right. Many hailstorms form in an area called Hail Alley, in the USA. The largest hailstones fall in the tropics.

▲ Rime ice forms a feathery white coating on objects.

Types of ice

Different types of ice can form in an ice storm. One type is **rime**. Rime is a collection of ice crystals that coats the sides of tree branches and other objects facing a cold wind. The feathery rime is lighter than other kinds of ice. The ice crystals in rime form quickly and stick together. Because the crystals form so quickly, air is trapped inside them. The trapped air makes rime look white instead of clear.

Another type of ice is **glaze**. Glaze ice is a thick, clear coat of ice. It forms when rain from a warm layer of air above the ground falls into a thin layer of colder air nearer the ground. As it falls, the rain is liquid. But once it strikes the ground or objects on the ground, it freezes, forming a slippery glaze, or coating of ice.

Frozen rain is another type of falling ice. As the rain falls, it moves from warm air through a thicker layer of cold air. The cold air is at freezing point or below. The freezing point is the temperature at which water freezes, or 0°C. This temperature makes rain freeze while it is still in the air, turning it into solid pieces of ice. Frozen rain falls as wet, slippery, clear ice that bounces off the ground. These pieces of falling ice are smaller than hailstones, and are known as soft hail.

▲ Hailstones can pile up into large drifts like this one.

What are hailstorms like?

Thunderstorms may form during warm parts of the year and at the warmest time of day. Besides thunder and lightning, these storms can also produce strong winds and hail, or hailstones. Hailstones are solid chunks of ice at least half a centimetre across that fall from storm clouds.

Hail usually falls from a thunderstorm in columns called hailshafts. These columns move along at speeds of up to 97 kilometres (60 miles) per hour. The area of ground covered in hail after a hailstorm is called a hailstreak. Hailstreaks can be from 30 metres to more than than 30 kilometres (20 miles) wide. Hailstorms begin and end suddenly. They usually only last for about fifteen minutes.

People can tell when hail is falling. Large hailstones can crash into each other as they fall, making clicking sounds. Hailstones hit the ground or objects on the ground and bounce back up again. All of this crashing and bouncing is noisy.

If many hailstones fall at once, they can pile up together in large **drifts**. A drift is a pile of sand, snow or hailstones formed by the wind. Drifts of hailstones at the foot of hills have been known to reach up to 1.5 metres high.

▲ These hailstones have fallen from the cloud fading into the distance.

Hailstones

Hailstones have different shapes. Most hailstones are round, while others are oval like eggs. Some have irregular, lumpy shapes. Some hailstones are clusters with uneven edges. A cluster is a group of small hailstones that have frozen together.

 Sometimes winds blow small animals and other objects into clouds where hailstones are forming. These animals or objects can be covered by layers of ice and become part of hailstones. Some people have found hailstones with frogs, fish or turtles frozen inside them!

Each hailstone is made up of many layers of ice. Scientists have found hailstones that have up to 25 layers. If a hailstone is sliced open, the middle looks a bit like the inside of an onion. Some of the layers are white and some are clear ice.

During weak thunderstorms, the hailstones that form are small. During powerful storms in the tropics, hailstones the size of tennis balls or even grapefruit may form. These fall from the sky at speeds of up to 50 metres per second, destroying crops and greenhouses. In the UK, the last hailstorms with tennis ball-size hailstones were in 1958 and 1959.

Compared to raindrops, hailstones are hard and heavy. Small hailstones usually melt quickly. Large ones break windows, damage buildings and dent cars. They can also kill people and animals.

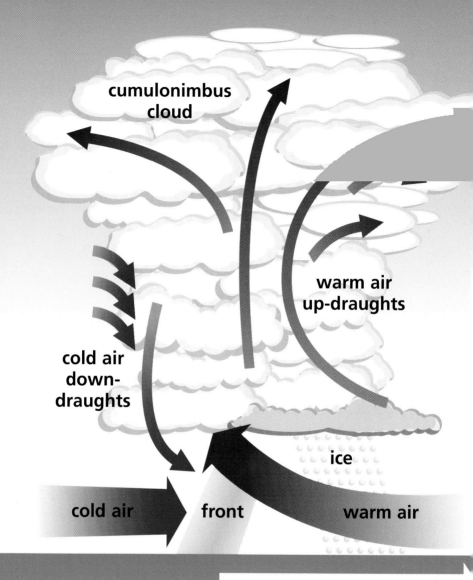

cumulonimbus cloud

warm air up-draughts

cold air down-draughts

ice

cold air

front

warm air

land

direction of storm travel

This diagram shows how an ice storm or hailstorm forms.

Causes of ice storms

Almost all storms happen when large masses of air meet. An **air mass** is a body of air with the same temperature and amount of **water vapour** throughout. Water vapour is water that is in gas form.

When a cold air mass and a warm air mass meet, they push against each other. If a cold air mass pushes a warm air mass upwards, it creates a cold **front**. If a warm air mass pushes against a cold air mass, it creates a warm front. Ice storms and hailstorms can form when fronts collide.

How ice storms form

Warm air holds more moisture, or water, than cold air. Warm air also weighs less than cold air. So when a warm air mass meets a cold air mass, the warm air mass rises above the cold air mass. As it rises, the warm air mass cools. The cooling air cannot hold as much water vapour. Tiny water droplets form. These droplets fall from the sky as **precipitation**.

All ice storms form in cold winter weather. The storms often begin as a warm front moves into an area with cold, dry air. As the warm front moves in, it pushes cold air ahead of it. The cold air makes the ground and other objects cold, too.

A storm forms when a cold air mass and a warm air mass meet. The cold air pushes the warm air up high above the ground. Rain forms in the warm air as it rises and cools. For an ice storm to form, there must be rain. As the rain falls, it passes through several layers of air. Each layer has a different temperature. Cold layers near the ground cause the rain to freeze.

▲ **Raindrops have splashed against this tree and frozen.**

Ice storms can also happen when wind blows very cold raindrops against cold objects. The first part of a raindrop that strikes a cold object freezes first. The rest of the drop splashes to the sides and also freezes. When this happens on road surfaces, it makes driving very dangerous.

▲ Hailstones are different sizes, depending on how many times they rise and fall in the clouds.

How hailstorms form

Hailstones form inside huge, dark cumulonimbus clouds. A cumulonimbus cloud is tall and filled with water and ice particles. The cloud becomes darker as more water vapour inside the cloud condenses into water and blocks the sunlight.

A cumulonimbus cloud is so tall that it is very cold near the top. Winds inside the cloud are very strong. **Up-draughts** push air upwards into the cloud. **Down-draughts** blow downwards from the top of the cloud to the bottom.

Hailstones form when tiny ice crystals in the cloud become coated with water. An up-draught carries these crystals into colder layers of air at the top of the cloud, where the new layer of water freezes. Then down-draughts carry the ice particles back to a lower part of the cloud. More water sticks to the ice particles before an up-draught blows them back up into the cold air again. Another layer of ice forms on the particles.

This up and down process can be repeated many times. The ice particles grow larger and larger. They become so heavy that the up-draught can no longer hold them up in the cloud. The chunks of ice fall to the ground as hailstones.

The larger the cumulonimbus cloud, the stronger the up-draughts and the bigger the hailstones can grow before they drop from the sky. By cutting open a hailstone and counting the layers of ice, you can work out how many times it travelled up and down inside a storm cloud.

Hailstones can flatten entire fields of crops in seconds.

Ice storms in history

Hailstorms flatten 8 to 10 per cent of the crops that grow in Hail Alley, in the USA, each year. The loss of these crops costs farmers millions of pounds. The farmers call hailstones the 'white plague' because they are so deadly to crops. A plague is a deadly disease.

Hailstorms also harm property. In just a few minutes, large hailstones can seriously dent thousands of cars, smash windows and crack tiles on roofs. Aeroplanes flying through hailstones have suffered so much damage that they could not be repaired. In December 2002, the landing of the space shuttle Endeavour was delayed while severe ice storms struck the eastern USA.

Safety during storms

A single ice storm can leave millions of people without electricity or heat. Fallen electricity cables crackle with sparks. They can kill anyone who comes too near. Heavy ice also makes roofs cave in and trees fall down.

People can stay safe during ice storms and hailstorms by being aware of the weather. They should watch weather reports on television or listen to news on the radio. They should listen out for special storm watches and warnings.

People should stay inside during hailstorms, especially when large hailstones are falling. They should move animals and cars under shelter. If people are caught in a hailstorm and cannot find shelter, they should cover their heads. People should never run out into a hailstorm to collect hailstones.

People should be very careful during and after ice storms. Driving on icy streets is difficult, so people should not drive. They should stay away from fallen telephone or electricity cables. People should also stay away from icicles and icy trees. An icicle is a long piece of hanging ice formed as dripping water freezes. The ice can fall on people and hurt or even kill them.

Avoid walking under large icicles. They may fall and hurt you.

People who live in cold places often carry survival kits in their cars. A survival kit should include first-aid supplies, warm blankets, food and water. A kit may also contain matches, candles, a torch and a bright piece of cloth to use as a signal in case the person needs to be rescued. Bright colours will show up well when everything else is covered in white snow and ice.

Deadly ice storms and hailstorms

One of the deadliest hailstorms in history struck Moradabad, in India, on 30 April, 1888. Hailstones the size of cricket balls hit many people. More than 230 people and hundreds of animals died.

In November 1921, one of the worst ice storms in US history struck Worcester in the state of Massachusetts. During this storm, glaze more than 5 centimetres thick froze on the ground. More than 100,000 trees were damaged or destroyed by the weight of the ice. Electricity cables also fell down and left the city without power for several days.

On 3 September, 1970, a major hailstorm hit Coffeyville, Kansas, in the USA. The largest recorded hailstone in USA history fell that day. It was about 19 centimetres wide and weighed 0.75 kilograms.

From 5 to 9 January, 1998, a large ice storm struck the north-east US and southern Canada. Trees, telephone lines and electricity cables were coated with a thick layer of ice. When electricity cables fell, more than 3.5 million people lost their power supply. Many people had to move into shelters. The storm caused more than £1400 million worth of damage in Canada and the USA.

▲ This car slid off an ice-coated road during the 1998 ice storm in North America.

Severe ice storms hit the eastern USA in November and December 2002. Hundreds of thousands of homes were left without electricity, as trees covered in ice fell on to electricity cables. Roads and railways were blocked and airports closed. At least twenty people died as a result of the storms, and more homes were left without power than after Hurricane Hugo in 1989.

Meteorologists look at satellite pictures of clouds, like this one, to find weather fronts.

Studying ice storms

Meteorologists are scientists who study the weather. Some meteorologists study ice storms and hailstorms. They try to find out the reasons why these storms begin.

Meteorologists use many tools to study the weather. **Satellites** are useful tools for meteorologists. Satellites are spacecraft with scientific instruments on them. They take pictures as they orbit the Earth. They then send the pictures back to the Earth. Meteorologists study the pictures to find fronts and air masses that might cause storms. They also use Doppler radar. Doppler radar uses special energy waves called radio waves to detect a storm's strength and the direction in which it is moving.

The future

Meteorologists use the information they gather to make weather **forecasts**. Forecasts are educated guesses about what a weather system might do in the near future. Meteorologists are trying to discover better ways to forecast ice storms and hailstorms. They hope that this will help save lives.

Scientists are working to keep roads safer during ice storms. Today, people spread salt on roads to melt ice. However, salt eats away at roads, bridges, cars and lorries. Scientists are trying to find different things to melt ice.

Ethylene glycol is one chemical that scientists have studied. It melts ice, but it also harms wildlife, so most people do not think it should replace salt.

Scientists are also studying another chemical called calcium magnesium acetate (CMA). CMA does not harm wildlife, but it is very expensive. Scientists are looking for cheaper ways to produce CMA. They hope that one day CMA will help to keep drivers safe by melting ice on the roads.

Because hailstorms cause so much damage, some scientists look for ways to change storm clouds and stop hail forming. A chemical called silver iodide can be added to clouds to stop hailstones from

▲ **Smaller hailstones do less damage to crops, property and people.**

getting so big. Small hailstones don't do as much damage to crops. But meteorologists know that they cannot prevent most ice storms and hailstorms. They can only warn people when these storms might strike. Today's powerful tools help meteorologists warn people earlier. People can stay safe by listening out for warnings and learning more about the weather.

Glossary

air mass body of air with the same temperature and amount of water vapour throughout

down-draught downwards-blowing wind

drift pile of hailstones, snow or sand formed by the wind

forecast educated guess about what a weather system is likely to do

front edge of a large air mass where it meets another air mass

glaze coating of ice caused by freezing rain

meteorologist scientist who studies weather

precipitation form of water, including snow, ice and rain, that falls from the sky

rime ice crystals that coat the side of objects facing a cold wind

satellite spacecraft that orbits the Earth; some carry special scientific instruments

up-draught upwards-blowing wind

water vapour water in the form of a gas

Addresses and Internet sites

Met Office
London Road
Bracknell
Berkshire, RG12 2SZ

Met Office Website
www.metoffice.gov.uk

BBC Weather Centre
www.bbc.co.uk/weather/weatherwise/factfiles/
    extremes/storms.shtml

Clouds R Us.com
www.rcn27.dial.pipex.com/cloudsrus/hail.html

Commonwealth Bureau of Meteorology
www.bom.gov.au/lam/climate/levelthree/c20thc/
    storm2.htm

Index